PHILOGOS / Tabula Rasa

On the Manifest Need for Fundamental Philosophical Redirection

by **Somos**

A consistent, comprehensive, rational and consequent worldview and universal perspective.

~The Truth Be Told~

Library of Congress Cataloging-in-Publication Data

SOMOS, date.
PHILOGOS/Tabula Rasa : On the Manifest Need for Fundamental
Philosophical Redirection / SOMOS – 3rd ed.
                                                    p. cm.
Includes bibliographical references.
978-0-9790859-0-1 : $12.50 (est.)
1. Philosophy.   2. Religion—Miscellanea. I. Title.
BF1999.S5728 1989
191—dc20   89-80842
                                                    CIP

THIRD EDITION

Manufactured in the United States of America
ISBN: 978-0-9790859-0-1

Library of Congress Catalog Card No.: 2006936498

0 9 8 7 6 5 4 3 2 1

Distributed to the trade by
AtlasBooks

To world literature
And toward a time when
Ultimate truth and enlightenment
May become more widely sought and understood.

*

These are not *conforming* views, rather, they invite you to think for yourself and find your place in the maze of this, your life.

Ever since ancient times, man has sought to understand the world around him, from the deep, distant universe to the ever smaller probes in biology. Problem is, early on those in control, the initiated, made their carefully honed religious 'findings' their own 'truth', guided by their emerging hierarchal elites—resulting in religious and cultural dominance over the unsuspecting, dormant masses who became subject to teachings with little or no regard to deeper understanding. The focused selection process in the ultimate choosing of the biblical gospels over all other gospels that had been written, including the gnostic gospels, must be seen as a glaring example of their 'insider' workings, as are the wanting traditional practices of the Roman Catholic Church, and of the Islamic faith, to this day. The consequence being that without wider, deeper understanding and humility, humanity has embarked on more wrong paths than can be imagined.

This book tries to illuminate the ordinary man's access to real fact and truth that has been withheld from him for so long by the old, traditional, 'accepted' establishments.

*

CONTENTS

FOREWORD

Philosophic Reflections

San Diego has its world-famous zoo. Besides being a most beautiful botanical garden, it boasts a multitude of animal species. Beings who, so far as we can tell with pretty final certitude, do not much ponder why they are there. They just *are*—without question nor wonder about why, nor for what purpose. All they seem concerned about or driven to is their food and procreation, plenty of evidence of that around the zoo, making sure their species survive. *Nature's plot? God's will and design?—Just that simple?*

Oddly enough, despite our advanced evolution, humans seem to buy into such simple concepts for their own being, as evidenced by the world's plentiful human population. Nevertheless, there is something that distinguishes man from animal. As a species, we humans have evolved a certain metaphysical trait, a spiritual need. We *need to know* about our "soul," we are drawn to dealing in some way with our *un-knowing, yet persistent awareness,* of a metaphysical "other side" out there.

Religion plays an important role in this, as illustrated by the early California Missions' history of more developed peoples bringing spiritual messages to aboriginal, native populations. But religion will soon ask or tell one *how or what to believe,* to believe a certain way, or else—depending largely on what religious environment one has been born into. Humanity is thus split into a multitude of different, limited belief systems. For open minds, and judging from our long, suffering history, this is not a rational process.

Enter philosophy. A process that, not unlike religion itself, has suffered also from serious setback in *human priorities.* So then, are we allowing ourselves to actually sink back deeper into the hopeless abyss of just the physical life in the flesh, closer to the zoo population in non-wonder about ourselves and creation, *away from the realm of metaphysical reality?* Or shall we come to welcome the dawn of renewed, fundamental philosophical inquiry and enlightenment after the dust of our modern, blinding high-tech life has settled?

Evidently, science and technology will bring us nearer and nearer the limits of comprehensibility—but in the end, neither will be able to *explain anything* about our true essential nature, our essential being, the nature of true reality, about rationality. *We need philosophical reflection, philosophical interpretation and understanding to sort it all out.*

PREFACE

www.philogos.org

Philosophy on this site is live and renewing, or as we would say in computer browser language, "refreshing," updating on our way to full understanding. We go from the basis of what is (now) *known as fact*, from our current understanding of things, and amalgamate it with our fresh, ongoing deep thought and inquiry for the attainment of new *realization*, new cognizance, and enlightenment.

Even the Catholic Church has come to the *realization* that traditional dogma is no longer the way to maintain course. Galileo and the Inquisition notwithstanding, the Pope tapped into 'fresh knowledge' once again to conclude that *"fresh knowledge leads to the recognition of the theory of evolution as more than just a hypothesis."* This offers renewed hope of bringing the religious and reasoned approaches of inquiry into fact and truth closer together.

Holding to the premise that **Religion and Philosophy** will ultimately interact in bringing forth consequential answers to the mystery of our being, we combined the
search for wisdom, Philosophy, with the *religious Logos*
to coin our name, and our internet identity: **Philogos.org**—
The subtitle 'Tabula Rasa' addresses our need to back off
the myriad time-*dis*honored belief systems, faiths, voices
and opinions that have hindered our access to the shrouded
deep truth so long and have brought us to the brink of
violent self-destruction. *We simply must reduce the be-
wildering multitude of beliefs and faiths to a basic, overriding, ubiquitous level of truth that everyone can sign on
to in good faith.*

   *The attainment of enlightened 'realization' of fact
and truth about the phenomenon of material, physical
and temporal manifestation is our stated purpose, aim
and objective.*

   *In this effort, however, we cannot subscribe to any
dogmas, preconceived notions, or traditional belief systems for tradition's sake. We need to seek and find fact and
truth no matter where it may take us, and as we find it, we
must recognize and defend it for what it is, and must be:
the stand-alone fact and truth. Not your truth, not mine,
but what has to be the total, overarching fact and truth.
We must be sure to make a distinction between 'generic'
truth and 'fact and truth' so that a generic truth concept in
search of the real thing is not let to wander back into the
wide wasteland of opinion, pretense, hypocrisy, and all
manner of wrong interpretations instead of reaching for*

*the intended realm of real fact and truth. Every being has
its own, individual inner mind structure or level of awareness from which it looks out and sees, perceives things. For
the true seeker, the crux lies in his rising above his own self
and looking at the total 'bigger picture'.*

*We hold ultimate truth as being singular and absolute,
and mere fragmental shades of it as in pursuit of extraneous
causes must not be imposed upon the human psyche super-
stitiously, whether by religious zealotry, hypocrisy, pretense,
deception or any other means of overpowering, including
physical violence and—yes, ignorance. When it's all said and
done, the bottom line will emerge in the metaphysical realm,
in a big way.*

For thousands of years, we humans have pondered
our being, our origin, our fate, our purpose.

Do you think the Grand Canyon, or Mount Ever-
est, or the vast oceans have ever pondered such questions
about their being (there)?

Obviously not, and therein lies one important aspect of our answers to the great puzzle.

Recorded human **awareness** of something *other
than the being in the flesh*—of the metaphysical, spiritual
if you will—started about four millennia ago with Abra-
ham and our oldest of religions. Following 'soon' after,
Eastern religions made their metaphysical entry. The
Western world began its calendar count with the Christian event teaching the spiritual life.

Earliest recorded **philosophy** generally lagged behind
these religious forerunners. Somehow not quite satisfied

with just the religious (belief) systems, true philosophy sees the human situation, and existence as a whole, as a deeper challenge and seeks to find answers *based on reasoning things out.* However, the convenience of the status quo and the advent and promise of untold technological and lifestyle advances have more recently all but blinded the human drive to delve deeper into man's basic being, into his essential nature, his meaning, his significance— threatening to make self-discovery and philosophy an 'endangered' pursuit, even as the serious influence of some religions is declining as well.

'Doing (modern) Philosophy' can mean many things— in most instances, though, it means not much more than the busying with what earlier thinkers had said, often long ago. It seems the longer ago, the more mythical the nature of those early thoughts. As stated before, we want to deal hand in hand, *firsthand* with **update knowledge, awareness and understanding** for the attainment of *new realization,* rather than with indeterminate conjecture from long ago, doubtless still subject to inherent archaic preconceptions and traditions. It is our aim to base our philosophical inquiry upon *rationally recognized, known fact and truth, and upon a clean slate*—Tabula Rasa—without prior notions, superstitions, presuppositions, or hypocrisy.

REALIZATION IS THE STEPPING STONE TO ENLIGHTENMENT

AUTHOR'S COMMENTS

This publication should not be critically acclaimed or critically condemned. It is simply an effort to help understand, recognize, define—fundamentally—our actual true nature and that of all things.

You can contribute by defining, stating things better, differently, the way *you* perceive them. Remember, though, we are in the arena of philosophical inquiry. We are not into science, religion, or whatever one's inclination may be. We are into independent, neutral, philosophical inquiry.

What do you think, fundamentally, this universe is all about?

That is the question. Again, please do not respond that Allah is great, that God is almighty, or that you do or do not believe in a creator, and that when it is all over, we are going to be in Heaven (or in Hell, as the case may be). Or that eventually, through science we shall be able to know all there is to know about the physical universe. For if we knew it all at this very moment, even with all that knowledge, we still would not have an answer to the *fundamental question of what its rational purpose and moral objective might be.*

So far, all we may know and conclude for certain is that this universe is about *something—but what?*

Our ultimate fulfillment is not in our better knowledge of technology, in a more developed, 'modern' way of life, or in our adherence to one of the many intangible belief systems handed down to us. *It is in our coming to truly understand the nature of that certain SOME-THING, in our basic realization of our true selves,* of our wanting essential nature, of our very creature life—and in our ultimate transcendence through the recognition and acceptance of higher universal truth principles.

Why do some of us ask these questions?
Why do some of us go to church?
Why are some of us hardened, uncaring criminals?
And why, oh why, do most of us just live a humdrum,
'content' yet unfulfilled, fearful, uncertain life
—not asking, not knowing, not understanding—
seemingly not caring about much other than their
own, immediate little selves and self-interests?

There are answers to these questions, and we shall try
to wire the reader for some comprehension and
understanding of them.

Why wilt Thou distance Thyself from Us All and from our Opinion?
"I write not to please you, but that you should learn something."
—Goethe

To You—The Reader:

Do you see the need for fundamental philosophical redirection manifest?

For if you do not, if you are 'happy and content' with the way you are and see things and feel no psychological, inner, spiritual need for change, no need for our deliverance, then we really have very little to talk about. You can go back quietly to the routine mind-set of your children, your church, your job, your national purpose, your physical world, procreation, and continue the human experience on the familiar, circular path.

Never even mind our long, sad history—just consider that in this, our time alone, fallacious, imperfect, wanting human aims, interpretations and understanding have brought on conflagrations with our entire world at war against itself. And no sooner a conflict 'settled' than humanity has raced on to amassing ever more deadly weapons, supposedly to 'settle' yet the next conflict. Only by now, we may just 'settle all', right into complete annihilation and oblivion. Oh, what clear proof of fundamentally wrong premise in human pursuit and *un*enlightened endeavor.

To be sure, our physical oblivion is preordained all right, but it better be to the upside through higher awareness, for higher purpose, and not for the sake of worldly, physical objectives and greedy destruction. For if we do not get out from under the yoke of the physical world with 'graduation papers', with higher spiritual awareness, our lower energy will surely have to stay put in an imperfect state from which to eventually work its way up and out. There is no way we can reach a coveted higher, non-physical, spiritual level of existence with low and wrong impulses in our hearts and subconscious souls. That is already manifest, isn't it? For we are here now in an imperfect state—predisposed low spirit created this, the physical, the temporal, us, before! How easy, how straightforward it would all be if only we recognized our basic problem, if only we could see ourselves prepared to accept and follow through consequentially on those higher principles of true reality—that of infinity, of eternity.

Material, physical considerations are not at the core of our needed redirection. To be sure, social order, righteousness, security, and economic freedoms have their place as we prepare for our way home, but our real and highest values lie in the pursuit of our true destiny: the achievement of deepest spiritual maturity and awareness in our subconscious—and the resultant tangible transformation to a higher essence of existence.

. . . and whoever strives for perfection strives for something divine.
—Michelangelo

Certainly, it is
heaven on earth
to have one's mind
move in charity,
rest in providence, and
turn upon the poles of truth.

—Francis Bacon

INTRODUCTION

Where We Stand

When it comes to our real destiny, we still perceive much like the wild tribe in the jungle that is waiting on top of the hill by their bamboo-build airplane replica, praying for another airplane to appear in their 'heavens' to save them—except that in our 'civilized, cultured' traditions, we look to *our* various religious memorabilia for props instead.

In the case of the tribe, a 'real' airplane had once in fact appeared in their skies, dropping food and supplies for its starved people. Their comprehension, or awareness level, though, could not fathom the *realization* that fellow human beings were actually behind their 'miracle', so they continued 'believing' in a concept they could muster—that some abstract providential 'God' had come to them from the heavens with help. And now the hungry tribe hopes and prays on the hill every day for *their God's* return.

Well, we know better, don't we?

Evidently, we don't.

In our own ways, and perhaps hypocritically, we cling to our old beliefs that simply are no longer relevant and in step with our higher comprehension level. In the process, something is going awry—perhaps more than we realize and are willing to admit. Public morals and ethics are no longer supported by a fully *accepted* belief system, and there is nothing tangible to replace the old values. "Values" that, alas, had once more likely been accepted as much in fear, ignorance, uncertainty, and imposed superstition as for their true values. Nonetheless, we have not seriously considered alternatives. Status quo establishments are comfortable saying "yes, yes" to the old and traditional, and we follow merrily along in those manifestly out-comprehended old ways. All the while, we need look no further than the Inquisition to see how our higher comprehension and awareness levels can and do overtake traditional beliefs. Remember Galileo? No matter how noble, how ancient and durable our various beliefs may be and may have been, they smack of handed-down tradition, status quo, blind acceptance, superstition and error, even misguidance, fabrication and deception. The need cries out for bringing *our accepted faith in line with our direct belief in cognized true, moral and rational reality.*

Thus the time has surely come for us *to go with the blessings of our higher awareness and comprehension,* and to seek a new solemn standard of belief and faith in the true and the good and rational, in accord with our update knowledge and understanding.

We must probe not only the visible, physical forms and manifestations that are more appropriately the province of science anyway, but especially that beyond touch and sight—the metaphysical. For we must replace our old belief systems with new truth values, shed of any and all superstition, archaic tales and fables, deceptions and 'sacred', fallacious hand-downs.

A poignant example of prevalent contradictions with respect to real, true values is young children's perception of Santa Claus. How is it that those children become aware by about six years of age that they no longer really believe in the touching story of Santa . . .? It ceases to be acceptably real to them, it's a fable! And yet, after thousands of years, we still believe in the equally unlikely fables of immaculate conception, physical resurrection, or the wholesale salvation of human souls through the physical medium of "His" blood—all of which certainly not spiritually, divinely inspired. Let us not hear vain counter arguments that it is all meant metaphorically— there is nothing metaphoric about going along with such a superstitious bargain proposition as having Jesus pay for all our sins. It is too important an issue to weasel around the fact and truth of it, which is, of course, that we are indeed responsible for our wrongs. Can't accept the thought of having to be responsible for your own sins?

Instead, become a true, good Christian and stand up for all your transgressions, evil thoughts, deeds and intentions. Let the good of Jesus be free of all *our* faults and shortcomings, and have us share in the heavy burden of universal guilt, if we truly love him and his *spiritual message*.

And we'll soon find ourselves in a better world. One in which hypocrisy is not blurring our vision of the true facts.

We may know ever so much about many things, but if we fail to understand our own true nature and that of all things, then we cannot truly understand much of anything—above all, anything that could give us hope for deliverance.

PROLOGUE

Tabula Rasa—pure, clean slate!

That is the principle by which we want to set out and conduct our inquiry into the deeper questions of existence. No preconceptions, no prior notions, superstitions, archaic traditions, no deception, ignorance, hypocrisy, no spoils—just the facts, the real, reasonable and rational facts as we have come to know, comprehend and understand them, with our best faculties applied.

We have come a long way since realizing that the earth is *not* the center of the universe. But we have got to finally now go on to *separate all fiction from fact,* true reality from all that stuff of myth, of old convention and the (unreasoned) imagination. Then, come to grips with the *like realization of the way all things really are, fundamentally,* and go forth in fuller enlightenment.

We have had the flat earth and "it-all-came-about-in-seven-days" theorists, the Santa Claus and varied other stories, as well as the "believe-it-or-go-to-hell" groups. Not to speak of the ancient god figures of Egypt, the fledgling thinkers of Greece, and the Nirvanas. But we are now hundreds—well, thousands of years after all

that. We ought to be able to recognize, define and understand the true nature of things a lot more clearly by now. So let's see where update, rational, reasoned *realization and awareness* buck up against all that mushy, murky world of myth and make-believe.
In the end, our great surprise will be in the simplicity of it all.

Only astronomical evidence and reasoning from simplicity could carry the argument.

"But still, it (earth) moves."

Galileo Galilei, 1564–1642,

Upon being sentenced by the Roman Inquisition for realizing and supporting true reality,
that is, earth moving around the sun, and not the other way around.

ON THE ULTIMATE ESSENTIAL, CONSEQUENTIAL

In search of the ultimate criterion for finding true purpose and rationality in physical being and existence—toward understanding what it's all about—there are mighty few disciplines to turn to, really. There are Science, Religion, Philosophy (reflecting, reasoning, deducing, concluding); and then there is Hocus-Pocus, and—can *you* think of *any* other discipline that might cloister life's ultimate secrets, purpose and promise?

We might start by deliberating the gamut of science's findings, or by going into exhaustive religious discussions—but let's first take an overview of what we are trying to accomplish. Ultimately, should we *really* expect our answers to come from science's deep-seated last secrets, or from near-perfect delusion and edicts expressed in religious rites and traditions? *Or,* all considered, would it not be more appropriate and important for us to find *up front* whether it all is—*very basically, fundamentally*—rational, of good purpose, right or wrong, adequate or inadequate, in true essential nature? I opt for the latter.

If all the stuff of science, whatever it may yield for us, were not to measure up to 'good, adequate, moral and right', then we would surely have to ignore that discipline as one of our appropriate means of exploring the deep mysteries of existence. For in our proper, correct judgment, most assuredly *an ultimate good and right purpose* must be a paramount consideration, a prerequisite to any valid finding on the adequacy and rationality of being and existence. Science certainly has helped us like no other discipline toward understanding our tangible, physical world, but can it be the one to give us *ultimate* (metaphysical) answers? It is doubtful that it could deal with right or wrong, or even with rationality, as it appears very much in a class with inanimate phenomena, having no subjectivity of its own. It will do anything you want it to do, even in negative demonic patronage. Is the true ultimate criterion, then, an ethical, a moral question—in judgment over right and wrong, over error, ignorance and sin versus bliss and enlightenment? For us, a resounding *YES*—and with the right awareness, it is clearly a question of rationality as well.

Shall we go fishing on the lake this afternoon, or shall we go hunting in the woods? Is it a moral, ethical question? No, not for most. Instead, it is likely a question of preference, mood, or choice—of rationale only. But now ask the same question of a conscientious vegetarian. Reason alone might tell that vegetarian that it would be more fun paddling on the lake than to tramp through the bushes hunting. But to him, it cannot be a question of choice or preference in deciding between one and the other. It is, instead, an engulfing, overwhelming matter of conscience either way: killing another creature for his own physical sustenance—repugnant! The moral question, then, determines if he should engage in either activity at all—if in fact he would need any of science's knowledge, say, for the fishing gear, or for the hunting guns. Having decided beforehand on moral, ethical grounds that he has no use, no necessity for either, he can—in fact he *must do* rationally without the heavy hand of science altogether in keeping with his ultimate objective.

Rightfully, then—*in ultimate consequence*—the moral, ethical issue, right or wrong, good or evil, adequacy versus inadequacy, emerge as our final and rational determinants. The circle is complete when morality is in accord with rationality. Moral and rational, the correct combination—the way it ought to be, and is, when things are right.

It is my sure sense that it is this simple way with our life's last consequence—the ultimate criterion being a question of the rationality, of the morality, the adequacy of the nature of our being in light of highest universal principles—as the brief encounter with consciousness that is human life struggles toward its full self-realization.

ON RELATIVE "REALITY," REALIZATION AND TRUE AWARENESS

On this movie set, a two-man raft, trying to land on a re-mote island during a severe storm is being rocked back and forth between the boulders near the landing site . . . the two occupants have just confided in one another that they cannot swim . . . the excitement mounts. Will they make it, or will they crash against the nearest boulder with the next oncoming wave . . . and perish?

"The cameraman seems to hold nice and steady on his safe little platform," I say. To which the answer comes: "You don't have any imagination, no adventure in you—you can't go through life with your heavy foot on reality all the time!"

Reality—imagination, adventure?

It must be unsuspecting news to many, if not to most of us, that *our actual, conscious living reality* is the great-est adventure, the most exciting experience in our lives. To find true excitement, do we really need all that artifi-cial make-believe? Just try to summon up a vivid aware-

ness, not of the imagined, but of true reality, that you are
traveling through space on a small sphere (huge to us) at a
speed that would "blow all your imagination" if only you
could see it in its true reality. You are circling around a
star, and that star, our sun, circles around in yet a much
bigger space. And we are not standing on a "real" but in
actuality make-believe platform in a make-believe scene
for our observations. We are situated on the actual,
life-size reality of this globe, and we have within us a
mind that can make not only real, true observations, but
also reason out that which we are observing and experiencing.

"*That,* my dear, is true excitement, true adventure."
The actual, live experience of learning, of finding that
which is real, that which is ultimately true and consequential. For with all our *real* observations every passing
day, week, and year, we can come to new deductions,
draw new conclusions, and avail ourselves of the oppor-
tunity of getting ever a step closer to understanding our
being and the meaning of the universe—if only we care
enough to look for it.

I am truly excited about that which I have already
found, and about the hard and fast knowledge that I am
finding the deeper answers to this, our mysterious journey. How do I know? *I can see it clearly, in my mind, and
in the real world. Both are revealed to me all at once.*

Of course our dear little cat would not know what to
do with all that is being said here. She is very lovable,
hungry at eight in the morning, and hungry again at six in

the evening, sleeping half of her life away. Actually, not very different from many of our lives, is it? Just a bit of a difference in form and lifestyle—a horse race or similar diversion here and there, and a somewhat more complex way of life. Well, let's not overdo this comparison; after all, the cat is an animal, and we are . . . *human.*

But do you know in fact that in many, perhaps even in most cases, we humans *do* live surprisingly much in the same way—for the day, for the moment—never wondering what, in true essence, it is that makes things go round, but rather just satisfying our individual, mostly self-centered needs, wants, and desires over and over.

Now is this because so many of us just do not have in them much of what distinguishes human from animal, or is it because most humans simply don't care?

How could they not care *if they had the right awareness,* conscious or subconscious, to ask the timeless, deeper questions? Of course, as we shall see later, the telling truth is that in a *predisposed higher subconscious state,* life energy would not (have) become amalgamated with physical affliction, the flesh, the way we are, to begin with.

What kind of awareness, then, are we looking for? The awareness that would make us jump away from a falling rock?—No, our cat would probably do that much better. An Einstein's scientific grasp, awareness of something that not even he could *prove* to himself despite his "blind" understanding and comprehension of it? Or the awareness of a conscientious objector who realizes some-

thing most others don't, and it is a compelling force to
him?

What awareness is it that matters?

It is the awareness, the realization of our true essential nature and of the true nature of all things (by which
to determine our proper universal judgment and perspective).

In theory, rationally, we could spend the rest of our
time on the question of our true essential nature and yes,
perhaps, through such serious fundamental philosophical
inquiry alone, eventually make it home. But in reality, it
may prove too big a step, too great a metamorphosis to
undergo during one life span. For we are born as who and
what we are—yes—in our (subconscious) essential nature! And for most of us, the whole distance from here to
there cannot be overcome, our essential nature mutated—attaining full enlightenment—solely by rational,
logical philosophical deduction. *Deep, real understanding, true cognizance, and attained subconscious awareness* are prerequisites for our reaching the light, for our
transformation. As in the case of the genuine conscientious objector who may face severe punishment for his
action, he does not refuse military service because he has
just arbitrarily decided that he does not like things military, but because his *deep inner awareness and insight* tell
him in a compelling way that his participation in the military, in a deadly armed force, would be immoral, evil and

wrong. So *there,* then, is the difference between true *inner realization in conscience*—of real, deep cognizance—and an extraneous process of mere deduction without inner partaking or conviction as in the nature, say, of an expedient judgment or opinion.

Our capacity for the recognition and *realization* of our true essential nature and of the true nature of all things is closely tied to our innate makeup, deep inside us, in our subconscious realm. We are living the life of that essential nature, *of who and what that is*—that which we were born with as a result of our metaphysical predisposition—and the basic crux of it lies in our ability to attain the awareness of just *what, who* that is. Call it self-realization, if you will.

Curiously, even most highly educated, learned folks do not appear to be aware of, or admit to themselves, the thorough inadequacy of our human, physical existence in light of highest ultimate principles—of perceivable perfection (look for *"knowledge versus cognizance, understanding"* in chapter titled "On Original Thought, Ultimate Knowledge and Understanding.") While even our perfectly normal body is, in essence, 'a mess', it is afflicted man, unable to physically function on his own that proves the point more dramatically. And have you ever witnessed a complete autopsy, preferably in a state of deeper reflection and meditative contemplation?

That we do something, act, humble ourselves over the condition of our 'mess', of our imperfection, that is the message we get from our true, deep inner awareness through our conscience. All physical existence is innately inferior affliction, including our 'human being' as evidenced by just a brief critical look at our physical, flesh-and-blood, posterior-retentive anatomy. Supposedly having reached "Nirvana" but then going right on acting out and procreating its antithesis, physical life, is solid proof that such a purported "Nirvana" was in fact a mere Fata Morgana. A true Nirvana state will lead us to Paranirvana, the *knowledge that we won't be back in, or want to pass on, the flesh. Then we shall have in fact graduated up, and our deliverance from the flesh will have us predisposed for higher essential being.* (See also "On the Province of Human Judgment, Horizon and Philosophy.")

Now then, learning these principles and *developing in us that higher subconscious awareness, this is our real task, our true 'religion', our door toward salvation and deliverance.*

The way is through initially conscious effort, then in progressively acquired *subconscious awareness and realization.* Just keep watching, listening, observing, and reasoning. Inside and outside ourselves, through constant, meditative contemplation—until the depth of our subconscious is reached and penetrated. It is not something that can be accomplished as only a distant, passive side activity— it takes a firm, focused determination and persistent, mental/spiritual effort to apprehend, influence, and mutate our innermost self, our subconscious.

After gaining higher awareness and understanding,

and its absorption into our subconscious, we shall eventually emerge in a higher state of being, in a new essential nature, much like the adult who has grown out of wanting to play the children's games of marbles or hide-and-seek.

ON THE NATURE OF THINGS AND ON ESSENTIAL NATURE

Most of the existing, that which is, does simply that: it just *exists*, it just *is*. It never seems to bother to define itself; it's just there.

But to be sure, everything that exists, all there is, all that lives, is by virtue of its very existence, of its very being, a certain something. What that certain something is intrinsically, fundamentally, raises the question of essential nature.

What, who are we, essentially, in pure, ultimate analysis? Mortal, physical bones, flesh and blood—or a metaphysical essence, an energy using the physical container as its vehicle, its carrier? Which, actually, is our true essential nature—our physical manifestation, or the life, the invisible energy that is in this physical 'container'?

We have to consider all aspects. We cannot just study our brain, or the digestive system, or any or all of our physical body, even our entire human Genome, for final answers about ourselves. Our considerations are of a much deeper nature. When little birds, with brains to match,

have summer and winter homes in two different hemi-
spheres of our globe and have the wherewithal to find the
same building sites over and over again thousands of miles
away where they'll spend their next season—without a
compass, directions, or any kind of navigational aids as
we know them; when a little spider constructs a master-
piece of architecture in its web, then we have to look elsewhere than in our human, supposedly know-it-all,
"top-of-the-line" model for final answers. It appears that
this 'elsewhere' can be explained only by the presence and
interaction of a transcendent property in essential nature,
for it could not otherwise be fathomed how a newborn,
not yet developed, blind kangaroo young a mere couple of
inches tiny, 'knows' to look for and find its pouch *outside
the mother's belly, on its own*. And think about how newly
hatched birds practically 'fly' into their worldly existence,
and whales launch straight into water from their mother's
belly to become immediate aquatic experts. There are in-
numerable other examples in this process that simply cannot be explained away as being just physical happenings
only; there are, as we have to recognize, clear metaphysical influences at work here that transcend stand-alone
physical phenomena.

Alive, living, we are obviously something different
from when we are dead corpses. Dead, we are a plain
physical manifestation comparable to the rocks and boulders in the desert. The nature of the energy in that dead
body is merely mechanical, like that in other inanimate
physical phenomena. Thus, the difference between our

creature life—our live state—and our dead, inanimate state is the *(transcendent) metaphysical essence that dwells in us.* In other words, that essence is our basic and essential being, our essential nature, call it our 'soul', if you will.

So what should concern us is that invisible something, that live essence, that impulse that comes to the 'body' at conception, and leaves it at death. Concern over why it needed to be amalgamated with that 'mechanical, physical' phenomenon of a body in the first place. Yes, concern over and cognizance of that invisible something, that true essence of our being, our innermost essential nature: the subconscious energy that transcends the physical. Simply put, our essential nature is that which is deep within us; it is our subconscious, our 'invisible' self, our real life energy, our true reality. The invisible: a world in and of itself, transcending our physical 'being', but in it having an apparent temporal manifestation and form of expression.

Something missing here on the way toward explaining essential nature in all existence? Yes, like what the essential nature is of the poor little bird that finds its winter home at the other end of the earth. Or of our resident master architect, the spider. Of our busy ants. How about the essential nature of an oak tree, perfectly grown from its acorn seed? And of a rock quarry—and of the Grand Canyon?

By now we begin to sense that philosophically, essential nature is in some contrast to object, inanimate, passive physical phenomena—to the elements of nature, to nature itself with its genetically programmed, molecular processes. As the very name implies, essential nature denotes 'essence' in being. The *"Nature of Things"* is thus set apart from *"Essential Nature"*—the latter signaling the presence of an independent, metaphysical strain of living energy, eventually culminating in the physical worlds in self-cognizant, self-realizing, self-determining being.

The basic characteristic of a rock—as of any inanimate object—is that it is just that: a rock, a physical, object (energy) phenomenon. We might say it has in and of itself no independent essential nature or, rather, no subjectivity of its own. It is simply a "manifestation of nature," part of a "bigger picture" without its own will and living, determining essence.

The fact that object water freezes at 0° centigrade is hardly a matter of (its) *essential nature*. It is, rather, a process characteristic of the natural elements. Essentially, scientifically speaking, the water's components are hydrogen and oxygen (H_2O), but like most things in science, this does not explain H or O fundamentally, philosophically. As it were, the stuff that H and O are intrinsically, separate and on their own, should perhaps better explain what water is, but as a practical matter, we commonly know even less about those components individually than we know about the water they form together. So as usual, solely scientific analysis does not take us very far by way of fundamental answers and explanation. (See a similar analogy in the "Physicist's Equation" chapter.)

Purely object (apparently unmotivated) energy manifestation—i.e., the passive, object world of physics, the world of the chemical elements, and of non-cognizant nature—must be the subject of a separate determination in our inquiry. These manifestations have no concern over religion or conscience—it therefore follows that philosophically, they can be dealt with by us only categorically, as opposed to subjective essential being in which self-realization and self-cognizance have occurred, resulting in self-accountability. In the latter, the responsibility shifts away from the "bigger picture" non-cognizant worlds to the self-cognizant, self-realizing being whose reasoning faculty, philosophic inclination, and resultant conscience become the accountable agency of decision, judgment, and determination.

Now all this should not be taken to mean that essential nature is completely lacking in the object, passive and non-cognizant worlds, for it is still a legitimate question to ask: *What is the essential nature of the Universe—and of everything in it?*

Yes, surely there is energy, essence even in a rock, and in the Grand Canyon, and in the tree and, of course, in our little bird. It's just that inanimate and non-cognizant existence have to be viewed and judged (by us) as a separate, overarching entity encompassing matter, space, time, all physical phenomena and non-cognizant, living 'nature'—as if it were all a helpless child unable to answer or speak for itself. *An independent philosophical inquiry and determination is due for this entity* as a whole, as its 'responsibility' is set apart from that of our own, cognizant essential nature (see "On Nature and the Object World" and "On the Categorical Judgment on the Non-Cognizant Worlds.")

Thus, the crux of it is that on the one hand, accountability belongs to a 'bigger agency' of responsibility, while on the other, us limited but conscious, cognizant, comprehending beings are responsible within *'our jurisdiction'*. In other words, if we will just define, know, and keep our proper place in this perplexing universal maze, we are going to get along just fine philosophically, and as a whole.

WE ARE ALL SINNERS

In universally accepted awareness, we recognize our shortcomings, our inadequateness, our imperfection, but we nevertheless insist on persisting as 'sinners'—yet all the while claiming, and truly believing, that we are "the greatest, *created in the very image of the perfect God.*"

There is a pious fellowship among man, of intended good will at that, in this acknowledged inadequacy—you can see it in the churches: the hand-holding, the singing, the chanting, "we are all sinners"—they know it. The contradiction is there, incontrovertibly, and that is one of the key puzzles we have to solve.

We are either of a perfect God—ordained, destined to aspire to 'perfectness', to 'come home' to a realm of perfection, abandoning our imperfect one—or we are forsaken as not of a perfect God, somehow misplaced in chaos, in a scandalous universe, condemned to an imperfect existence of wanting and suffering ad infinitum—as in fact we seem to perceive and perpetuate it for ourselves.

Which shall it be?

Behold, we are on the threshold of coming into the

greatest, delivering awareness—that of the conscious recognition, the full cognizance of the reality of our inadequacy under a perfect God's true, highest principles. Put another way, what we are discovering—what we are becoming aware of in our ongoing evolutional process— are the true, highest ultimate principles that we identify as a 'perfect God's.' Contrasted against them, we shall, given our new insight and higher awareness, see immediately that we fail to measure up, with or without the chanting in religious rites.

Remember the ancient stone cultures in earlier human history? In wide contrast, we are now moving toward a time of refined, *enlightened realization of nonphysical reality,* of the metaphysical, of the spiritual. Genuine, deep human insight shall eventually overcome all material symbolization of metaphysical reality, and physical anchors such as our elaborate churches and other monuments intended to aid in spiritual worship and in bearing witness to timeless, 'eternal' concepts will go the way of the true *spiritual insignificance* of such one-time sublime metaphors as the Egyptian pyramids, Stonehenge, or the Greek and Mayan temples. Remember always, God's perfect principles are formless, infinite, eternal, spiritual—*metaphysical,* as in fact the nature of morality is.

And so ultimate human fulfillment will not come through more and more complex, 'comfortable' lives and unimaginable gadgetries, but solely in *complete spiritual, metaphysical maturity.* In awareness on a level that will render being, existing on our physical plane a venture altogether passé, manifestly and resolutely incompatible with our new, deeper insight and self-cognizance.

Man, you who pretends to be searching
For the truth—you are not, really.

Instead, all you ever do is try to justify
Everything within and for yourself.

ON THE GOD CONCEPT

I wish someone could explain just *precisely* what they mean, exactly *what* they believe in, when they say: "I believe in God."

I cannot escape the feeling that they are unwittingly, unconsciously saying: I want to, *I need to* believe in an agency "to provide for me, to protect me from the (feared) unknown, to take care of my soul"—an insurance policy to look to for salvation and deliverance.

One of our great philosophers once put it a similar way: "Prayer—the begging—is the asking of God that which one is not prepared to do, to earn, for oneself." On Catholicism, he said: "The Catholic religion is a covenant to beg for entry into Heaven, which to earn for oneself, deemed too demanding, would be too uncomfortable—with the priests acting as instigating intermediaries," as clearly demonstrated by the confession process.

The concept of a God is all right. As a philosopher given to deep reflection upon what is real and true, I do not or cannot fault the concept of 'GOD' as a symbol of the perfect. I only take issue with the exhaustively many ways that *we perceive God to be,* that is, with the very erroneous notions we have on the subject. As just one example, an analogy comes to mind between Christian teaching and the cat that sniffs your pointing finger instead of paying attention to the indicated direction. As the cat does not understand the meaning of the pointing, its focus is on the physical finger itself because that is all it can fathom and relate to. So do devout Christians miss the true message when they focus for their salvation on the *physical flesh and blood* of the messenger, instead of actually *following in the (spiritual) direction pointed to.* This practice is a failed attempt at making the metaphysical, the spiritual communicable, comprehensible to the uninitiated by its personification in a physical medium.

God is what's right, that which is true, adequate, perfect, eternal and infinite—therefore, spiritual (metaphysical, non-physical). Consequently, if we want to be going in the direction of 'God' and seriously aspire to God-like, God-fearing being, then we have to become spiritual and pursue the timeless, the metaphysical, as opposed to continuing on in the temporal, phenomenal, physical realm.

Now, how can this rational contention be arguable?

It surely is a serious fallacy to attribute to a 'perfect God' the creation of a temporal, wanting physical universe when it is for certain the work of a negative power out to wallow, to conquer in the temporal, in the physical, the imperfect (see the chapters "On Eternity and the Temporal" and "Reflections.")

ON THE PHYSICIST'S EQUATION

$E = MC^2$ will never go anywhere with respect to a unified field theory because by its nature and intent, the equation does not go back to, it does not include, ultimate origin. To say that two things are equal does not begin to philosophically satisfy, explain what either 'thing' is and whence it came, and all the other questions of its reason, rationale, purpose, and ultimate destiny. There will never be a unified theory 'explaining everything' that does not figure in the original, eternal state whilst explaining away temporal, physical causation; it is, in fact, compellingly self-evident that unification is possible *altogether only in the original, eternal, polarity-less, perfect state.*

In true actual fact, but not as envisioned in $E = MC^2$, *E* accounts for immensely more than just the value in that equivalency. For energy, by virtue of its link to ultimate origin—the polarity-less, perfect energy state—does reach back to the original, eternal causation. However, as there is no place for that eternal, polarity-less, perfect state energy in our temporal, physical realm, no unification is ever possible on this level.

What has to be said about the physical universe, and therefore also about $E = MC^2$, physicist Einstein said best himself, stating: "What interests me is whether God could have had anything to do with it . . ." So he himself sensed, quite typically of the suspecting scientist, that the original, perfect, eternal state, which we shall call God's, was left out of the deliberations, particularly in this case, in his application as regards the equation. Still, he equated 'Energy', which in true reality is of the stuff linked to the original perfect state, with what only phenomenally, physically, temporally exists—Mass, times the constant in the physical world, the speed of light. Not good enough. Energy and its origin is, in quite a literal sense, *infinitely, eternally* more than just equal to that which is purely physical and temporal.

It thus follows that simply E = G, *Gravity,* would more adequately represent (primal, eternal) *Energy* to our metaphysical level of comprehension. Leaving out the temporal components, the physical (M), Mass, and (C), the Speed of light in a physical world, would certainly be a lesser shortcoming than to leave out, as in Gravity, the potential or, rather, *certain link to the true essence of everything: the non-physical, infinite, eternal, perfect energy state.* Gravity being effective to infinity should tell us without a doubt its link to that original energy, reaffirming the error in our assumption that suspected 'missing matter' may be the hidden "phantom gravity source."

To help your imagination along, envision first the

age of the Grand Canyon—*as we know it today—then back up further in time by the actual age of the deep rock formations themselves before the rise of the territory creating the high plateaus around today's canyon. Then, juxtapose those billions of years to the scientifically assumed distance of the universal "source" at the speed of light—some 12 to 15 billion (?) LIGHT YEARS FAR*—and imagine thus the gravitational energy required over that incredible distance to keep just the *known* universe in tow! Now *THERE*, then, is a (truly metaphysical) idea of the force, of the magnitude, of the *UNIMAGINABLE VALUE OF UNIVERSAL ENERGY* behind it all.

Invisible, untouchable as its mother—eternal, perfect state energy—*gravity* obviously then looms much larger in ordering the universe, atomically (infinitesimally) to cosmically (infinitely), than could ever be demonstrated by the MC^2 equation in that representation of, reference to, mere physical phenomenon. By itself—without the reign of that greatest universal force and leash of universal law, gravity—the physical universe would be hopelessly chaotic in all respects, certainly altogether incapable of existing as we know it.

At some point, infinity (and the infinitesimal) will transcend the bounds of physical phenomena, of our phenomenal worlds; this well beyond our province of empirical comprehension in either direction—hence our need for the *metaphysical,* and for unification needing to reach far beyond any one of our known disciplines, in fact craving for all of them to come together as a prerequisite to any hopes of our apprehending the goal and to begin perceiving ultimate reality. Therefore, not until we unify our religion, our science, and philosophy rationally in one fundamental, comprehensive, comprehending awareness and understanding about everything, shall we come close in concept to any realistic perception on field unification. See earlier for the bottom line on polarity-less, perfect state unification.

In man's quest to find real purpose,
there can be little doubt that he sees the
overriding mission of his existence in
the attainment of higher status than his own.

How long man is going to find that true
about himself while failing to initiate some real,
tangible steps toward his transition to
such higher level in essential nature,
is a matter of great curiosity and puzzlement.

The problem is that man insists on remaining in
his (limited) physical state of being, in "seeing,
hearing, touching, experiencing, controlling" things.
Doings that he cannot conceive of the higher levels
affording him, so he keeps groveling in his imperfect,
suffering, "controlling" yet helpless, hopeless state.

Once again, the key is in the total awareness of,
and knowing faith in, the true reality of the
higher level—which man evidently still lacks in
order to undertake those tangible steps off 'his pad',
and venturing on up and out of the physical realm.

ON SUBCONSCIOUS AWARENESS

We hear of meditation, of introspection, of going inside oneself. We know about consciousness and conscience, about right and wrong. Why do you think that is? And why are some of us drawn to it more than others?

We arrive on this scene on different levels, different frequencies of consciousness and awareness, you might say in different stages of wholeness, of perfection (or imperfection). Our bodies are carriers of energy—imagine it to be electric current. The higher the 'frequency', the sensitivity of that energy, the more 'perfect' the being, its essential nature quality.

Now then, how do we influence that quality, the frequency of that energy in us in order to grow in our consciousness, in our (subconscious) awareness?

We have done it for centuries—through religion, morals, ethics, and introspection—by listening to our reasoned judgment, to our conscience.

Religion, however, has not grown with us, it has become dogmatized and out of touch with genuine, deeper truth and therefore with our new, higher level of awareness. As a consequence—failing a needed redirection—we are left with just loose pieces of morals and of our own conscience, without a charted course based on an overall picture. Much hollow, meaningless materialistic chaos has descended upon us as a result.

It is certainly true that every thing, every being, every creature exists on its own, different level. And so it is also among humans that each one's consciousness, awareness, and comprehension is different, varying with our subconscious level, our essential nature, just as each of us is uniquely different from all others in outer appearance—no two really alike.

Our mission in life is to learn to improve this subconscious quality and awareness in us. For it is our subconscious that determines our true being: *who, what we are, essentially—and are going to be*—no hocus-pocus about it.

The learning process in this is like any other learning process. First, you must *want* to learn, then you dedicate yourself to learning, and once you grow in tune with increasing awareness, you will never want to get off your journey of inner discovery.

Our inclination, our quest to learn (or not to learn) may be predisposed within a particular life span. If the 'current' within us is in a declining cycle (as in a hardened criminal), it may be difficult to reverse that negative flow within the space of a mortal life. But under normal circumstances, given the proper conditions, environment, influence, and teaching, our minds should be in a receiving mode for moving towards spiritual development and attainment of deeper insight and awareness—first conscious, then subconscious. (See also chapter "On Our Time.")

ON ORIGINAL THOUGHT, ULTIMATE KNOWLEDGE AND UNDERSTANDING

The ancient classics did not experience philosophy as the mere 'learning' or 'recital' of others' thoughts and quotations. They *originated* thought, albeit fledglingly compared to knowledge and comprehension gained since. And so it is with us today, that if we want to find new, basic understanding, we too, from our new vantage point, must go back to original concepts, to fundamentals—again thinking things out to their original causes. That is what they were trying to do way back then in their own early fashion, and that is the true meaning of philosophy.

In our contemporary 'philosophy', have you encountered anyone lately dealing with those truly causal subjects? (Note contemporary *'philosophy'*, for *science* is often searching for ultimate origins.) Yet today, no longer are water, air, earth, or fire the subject of possible 'ultimate sources' of everything. These are for us now in the domain of known physics.

Thus we must finally now extend and unify our philosophical inquiry toward a true ultimate origin, a first causation, the true source of the physical, temporal universe as we know it, without brushing the question aside with some simple strokes of religious jargon or tradition, or some scientific 'explanation' of the make-up of physical phenomena.

As we know, science, from its physical footings, has long been looking for a "theory to unify, explain everything"—but in vain. The time, therefore, has come for us to go beyond the purely physical—into the world of the invisible, untouchable, of the metaphysical, the world of pure principle, of universal law, into the realm of the unseen, as that of Gravity.

When physicist Einstein conjured up his famous theories, he honed in on, sensed, comprehended and somehow understood the principles behind his visions. He did not actually *know*—only to learn the practical outcome of his understanding of things later in life when it was eventually verified in applied physics.

Einstein himself said that the imagination is more important than direct knowledge. We can likewise sense, hone in on, *intuitively understand ultimate consequence* in and of all things without a priori *knowledge* of a perceived metaphysical 'other side'. The whole ultimate picture is quite certainly beyond the realm of our brief empirical experience (and comprehension) anyway, so that we have to be content with the consolation prize within our reach: the ample, compelling evidence of all the *wanting alternatives* 'on this side'. Thus we can find the proper direction to ultimate, delivering truth intuitively and by deduction, provided we really want to know the truth. Simply put, by identifying everything that is imperfect on one (our) side, we can closely deduce the good, right, and perfect on the other side. (See also "On Imperfection and the Perfect State.")

Full, total knowledge of all historical and evolutional facts has always been 'out there' by virtue of its being *synonymous with the true, complete history of all things and events* as they actually happened from the first occurrence of a dust particle, of impurity in eternal 'space'. There is only one way it happened; there is only one way things have come to be the way they have—and therefore *can be*—it thus follows that there can be only *one* truth about it. The crux in all of this is that we are just not privy to, aware of that total history, that total *specific knowledge*. To what extent we ever will is a matter of the measure of our limitations, perhaps of our determination and ultimate *capacity* to know—to some extent perhaps of the imagination, conjecture, or even randomness—may be a combination of some or all of these, or some other yet unknown metaphysical phenomena or teleological insights.

What in reality then is *true knowledge* but the total history, a true rendering of the complete makeup of all facts, of all things and events from their first origins to their ultimate end? Could it not be said, then, that genuine knowledge is but *known fact, known truth?*

Now then, what if we knew that total history, every aspect of physical existence and its cause, source, and origin; its intent, purpose, and goal, its every minute fact? Would we, in our limitation, comprehend, understand what is really going on, and would we want to change things, would we be us, want to be us? If *"they"* knew, would "monkeys or ants want to be monkeys or ants?" Would *we* want to be monkeys or ants? I would venture to say that with full awareness, comprehension, and understanding on higher levels, we would want to be *us* no more than we would want to be the monkeys or the ants.

We might just hold free passes to paradise if only we could know and *comprehend* the full facts and truth as they surely exist—if only we could muster awareness, realization and understanding to such a wide, open horizon.

But in *our reality,* what do we really look for? Ultimate knowledge? As should be evident by now, that would not necessarily help us. I had just asked the question: "If we *knew everything,* would we still want to be here, as we are, or not?" Would we strive to change things? I sincerely doubt it, for *we know quite a bit already and, even with all that knowledge of ours, we have not changed much, have we?* So knowledge alone does not really answer our plight. What it takes is *genuine, deep, ultimate understanding and cognizance—with a generous dose of humility to accept the real and consequential truth about ourselves.*

Remember, Einstein did not 'know', but he somehow comprehended, understood things before he (or anyone else) *knew*. Just as earlier man did not *know* that the earth was round, yet somehow imagined, comprehended, understood it *before* having had actual, verified *'knowledge'*. So yes, we can understand, we can answer the deeper questions without having empirical knowledge about it—through reasoned understanding and comprehension. We can comprehend without knowing, but knowledge by itself can be meaningless without comprehension, understanding, and cognizance. That is what Confucius must have meant when he said: "When we know, and we know that we know, and when we do not know, we know that we do not know—that is knowledge." But he might just as well be quoted as having said: ". . . that is comprehension, that is understanding."

The trained dog 'knows' various skills, but does it really comprehend what is going on? When it knows to perform certain acts, it is not from 'knowledge' in the sense of Confucius' knowledge of comprehension, but merely as a result of its familiar, non-cognizant training. Its natural instincts, of course, are quite another matter, emanating from nature's genetic programming and essential nature properties covered elsewhere.

Ultimate, true understanding comes with comprehension, and we acquire it through the recognition, acceptance, and subconscious absorption of real, consequential, quintessential fact and truth.

ON THE PROVINCE OF HUMAN JUDGMENT, HORIZON AND PHILOSOPHY

As we search for fundamental fact and truth, it is philosophy, our highest discipline and reasoning faculty not beholden to preconceptions of any kind that is eventually destined to find the door to man's deliverance. *It alone* can judge for us *rationally* what is ultimately appropriate, right, adequate, determinant, consequential, and of true meaning.

In our ultimate enlightenment, though, it shall be *philosophy and religion together* that will join in a final symbiotic fix on these and moral values and reign over our acceptance, implementation, and defense of them, as in good versus evil, adequacy or inadequacy, consequence or inconsequence. This either as a result of enlightened understanding between philosophy and true religious, metaphysical insight, or in one triumphing over the other; specifically, philosophy over religion in a similar fashion as scientific awareness did at the time of the Inquisition—notwithstanding the sad historic fact that it

took the Roman Catholic Church hundreds of years to finally "allow" fact and truth to prevail, and to concur in
that which, by virtue of genuine knowledge, is
self-evident, absent any hypocrisy, superstition, distor-
tion, or deception. In other words, allowing an up-to-it
comprehension level to prevail over old, erroneous beliefs.

As for science, it will remain anchored in the 'dust'
of the physical realm that is its domain, but there we must
leave the eventual undoing, the 'de-creation', the dissolution of the temporal, physical universe (note well: *temporal,* so there be no doubt about our proper understanding
of this fact), the oblivion of it all—of matter, the elements, the stars, of the 'bigger picture' factor—to other
determinants, other powers and/or levels of comprehension, most likely even to a random process and chance.
Let's not reject this latter prospect too out of hand, for
even our automated bank-teller machines use the random
principle to achieve the very purposeful, precise,
close-to-our-heart objective of safely and securely dispensing our daily cash.

Other than in the sole, rational, ultimate light and
consideration of good or evil, of adequacy versus inadequacy, consequence versus inconsequence, how could we
really presume to ever judge, at best, much more than our
own human situation in the maze and huge scale of universal things and events?

What we *can* very reliably do within the stated pur-
view, though, is to reason out, sense, *comprehend and un-*

derstand the nature of the eventual course of events, of the final outcome and conclusion—*and therefore in fact foresee it based on our understanding of highest universal principles,* without actually 'knowing' it, or otherwise becoming beholden to a certain belief system, or some particular faith, about it. But again, precisely how it will eventually occur, physically, is for us—and most likely even for a higher power—forever behind closed doors. Like the demolition of a building by explosives, we can foretell, even cause the building's collapse, but exactly how it is going to fall, and precisely where every piece of debris will be placed in the end, is impossible to predict; it cannot help but be a matter of chance, of an absolute, utter random process when it occurs. To be sure, the process will follow precise edicts of natural law at all times before surrendering at the gates of eternal law.

The final outcome, the end result, the purposeful objective (as with the bank-teller machine the dispensing of our exact cash)—in this case the cessation of temporal and physical manifestation—is pre-ordained by highest ultimate principles, an outcome inevitable within the latter's self-fulfilling attributes and requisites of eternity and infinity.

It would be an exercise in empty futility to try to guess precisely how the physical universe is going to make its exit. That is not important; *instead, it is the invisible, non-physical realm of eternal principles, of eternal law, of original energy as manifested in universal Grav-*

*ity—it is, in sum, only the inevitable, delivering final out-
come, a return to the perfect energy state, that ultimately
matters.*

It is often said that people involve themselves in 'philosophy' because it makes them feel important. Does it
hold also, then, that the priest in the pulpit is preaching
his religion in order to 'feel important'? Is it really trying
to 'feel important' that makes one judge our religions as
not meaningful, satisfying enough, as not adequate in
light of ultimate consequence—leaving one unfulfilled by
wanting dogma? Or is it indeed deeper insight and fuller
comprehension that is preventing us from simply 'believing, accepting' a scenario handed down by old writings
and 'traditional' teaching?

Well then, other than religion or science to explain the
state of things, *where could we turn* for answers to—and
proper deductions from—our being, if not to philosophy?
And without 'feeling important' about it—as a matter of
fact, feeling more humble the more one turns to it, actually
in rather exact proportion to the depth of one's philosophical inquiry and understanding.

Philosophy, reasoning, has more to do with inner
perception than with outer appearances, loud noises,
and pretenses of any kind—or even with university de-
grees. It is the direct inner search for deeper understanding, the need and the urge in us toward greater purpose,
real values, and apprehending ultimate fact and truth.

True philosophy, our search for wisdom, is undoubt-
edly the noblest, highest of human endeavors.

All the while, there is good reason for us humans to feel inadequate, incomplete, imperfect. And there is something especially incongruent about those studied, learned, highly erudite ones among us who appear with such insight in their knowledge about all those stars out there and about the world of atoms and of particle science, but who do not seem to ever ultimately recognize, acknowledge, and feel compelled to act upon the inherent shortcomings of us creatures living three score and ten in abject (physical) dependence, in such obvious inadequacy in light of even the crudest concepts of cognizable perfection.

We can talk about it, can't we? Take a person after a 'sumptuous' meal and drink, detain him or her unconditionally for just a few hours, and you approach the physical, dungy 'human' problem. The subject is more freely discussed, without a blink of the eye, when on a less personal level, a sewage line by a lake or in a coastal city breaks, when a beautiful natural bay gets contaminated due to sewage spills . . . do you get the point? Very vulnerable, us humans. Remember our autopsy and our 'messy' anatomy, running counter to our 'Nirvana'?

Light years, or more to the point, those laws eternal, I much prefer—even without a university degree.

*In the deepest, ultimate sense,
there is no other judgment to be made
than over good or evil, as between
perfection and imperfection,
adequacy or inadequacy.*

*The good, moral, rational and perfect
will surely bear eternal consequence—and
evil, the irrational, inadequacy and imperfection
prove eternally inconsequential in light of ultimate
perfection.*

ON IMPERFECTION AND THE PERFECT STATE

Can we perceive, define, know perfection? Not just a casual, passing kind. Perfection, perfectness as an Absolute?

We certainly can—even express it mathematically, by deduction: X minus imperfections equals perfection. That means, take the present, or any state, remove from it all imperfection, and you end up with perceivable perfection. As an ideal, as a concept, as a model, certainly. But then, what is 'God', if not an ideal, a model?

Sounds simplistic? Not if you have difficulty finding, defining perfection in the absolute any other way, from the 'outside'. If one cannot define the perfect state, at least one would be in a better position to know and identify imperfection (with which we are more familiar). Thus, the perfect state can be apprehended through alternative deduction, and a fairly clear perception of absolute perfection can emerge. And as we begin to seriously care and learn to identify imperfection, the task of more adequately perceiving ultimate perfection becomes ever more clear.

The definition of imperfection, in light of perceived

highest ultimate principles, if honestly pursued, is really self-evident, and the removal, philosophically, of all such imperfection from a given state will point the true, honest seeker clearly in the right direction toward absolute perfection.

Then, as in a double check, by overlaying the criteria of perceived absolute perfection on our worldly, physical and temporal manifestations, we can judge without a doubt whether our world and our empirical experience here do measure up. So again, if we are truly sincere and care enough about the criterion of ultimate perfection, we can identify and know our proper direction with absolute certainty. To the degree, however, that we philosophically compromise this process, we compromise our relationship to the first origin and ultimate destiny—the perfect state model.

> *To need or not to need be*
> *our imperfect, wanting selves—*
> *That is the question.*
>
> *In full enlightenment,*
> *not to need be thus—*
>
> *That is the answer.*

ON OUR TIME

In human history, short as it is, there have been various epochs: the pre-historic experience, of growing awareness, religious awakening, of the Dark Ages, Renaissance, creation of classical music, literature, and so on. We are now entering an epoch of truly higher awareness, comprehension and realization in which old beliefs and superstitions are simply becoming lost for their lack of substance and sufficiency vis-à-vis our new levels of knowledge and understanding.

We must fill the vacuum thus left with fundamental, basic values, with *genuine religion* and belief in tangible truth—reflecting our new, higher level of awareness. With genuine knowledge and understanding prevailing, *without* 'make-beliefs', hypocrisy and superstition.

Values shall be properly placed, and population numbers diminish. We already see that happening: truly more aware, consciously developed peoples are partaking less in rampant population explosion. Reason shall prevail and rationality come to be recognized in the good, moral, adequate, and perfect. Mental, spiritual contentment shall rise as a forerunner to ultimate deliverance from physical bondage. This, however, will not widely happen in the foreseeable or even somewhat distant future; but in eons of time, ultimately, it is the inevitable direction and outcome.

Serious contemplation is needed to get it right. For the young, we have to provide good, unbiased open teaching and education, rather than continuing on with the indoctrination of old, traditional notions that are erroneous, divisive, and hard to remove once instilled in a child's heart, soul, and thereby conscience. While more people in our time, especially among the young, are blessed with enough true cognizance and awareness so as not to be apt to fully believe and accept some of the old, unconvincing notions 'taught' them, where should they turn for proper guidance, for credibility, believability, plausibility, and reaffirmation?

Where lies the real truth? Real religion? What is it we really want or should want? Are we accomplishing what we are here to do? Are we really ready—getting ready—for higher essential being?

We need to sit down and tangibly pursue it, figure it out once and for all, and deal with it seriously so as to change our life—meaning our actual essential nature of being. Through serious inquiry and contemplation and a firm will, aspiration, and determination to find and foster true cognizance, *and to act on the new awareness and knowing belief in ultimate, fundamental, essential truth.*

In these days' life of delicate 'refinements', can you see yourself wanting to live in the rough, backward days 'when the West was won', of the Dark Ages, of human sacrifices 'for God's sake'—albeit 'He' just an idle, lustful, bloodthirsty worldly emperor? Looking back from today's vantage point, those conditions are virtually inconceivable. The answer, therefore, must surely be a resolute NO—for we are much more cognizant, aware, and insightful now—'*we know better*'.

And so it will come to pass that in other, future time periods man will understand ever more about himself, his life—about the universe, about 'our' world—until eventually, we shall reach the full light and *not* want to "come back" to this level of being altogether, to continue on as we are now—*imperfect, wanting, temporal, and physical in basic nature.*

But to this day, most of us are still simply accepting our condition, our physical plight, particularly with all our modern gadgets and our lives' comfort gains, our hopes and expectations—and besides, in all this we feel smugly 'superior' to our elders and ancestors, while looking yet for better future 'gains', for more smarts, and in midst of all these distractions, we do not seem to have those basic, fundamental philosophical needs and questions any more. Not like the old classics, or even those monastics who sought to preserve real meaning by recording the Bible.

For two to two-and-a-half millennia, indeed not much real, deep, fundamental inquiry has occurred regarding our existence. We seem to have come to accept our being as is, no questions asked. "Technological, scientific progress" is the new motto and goal, while our technicians feverishly look to develop yet the next, higher-resolution TV screens and fancier, more powerful computers. But no more real questions. Sadly, bookstores have all but abandoned their section for true, meaningful 'Philosophy', *the ongoing, renewing, direct search for ultimate wisdom and reality.*

The other tragic thing is that as all our teachings on 'divinity' date back so many years to when man first became literate and sought meaning about life and started making a written record, they have become shrouded in a strange, hard-to-shake mysticism. We therefore have not much to revere and look to but those blurred old notions, while pretending to be fulfilled within ourselves and 'happy' with our ever-increasing comforts and hopes, albeit falsely based in the deeper context of real, true meaning and purpose.

Yes, the time has surely come now when we must reassess our universal standing and seek anew real meaning from our new 'plateau' of understanding. That, in a nutshell, is our message, our task.

*This is not about guidance on how to live best,
on the best social conditions, the best economic
system—but rather, it is on our search concerning
the fundamental role of universal existence and of
our human situation.*

*Our conclusions touch on our whole being,
and that of the entire universe,
on very basic existence as we know it.*

ON THE TRUE MAKER—DEITY OR IMPOSTOR

Ever since the beginning of human self-cognizance, there has been some belief or another in a higher authority, a creator of it all. After all, creation "had to be"—it's all here, isn't it? And if there was a 'creation', there must have been a *creator—in kind!* So goes conventional teaching and religion.

What if the 'creation' of the physical, of the temporal worlds was in fact the work of a creator of another kind, a force of the negative, of impurity? True deity, the eternal law of ultimate perfection, may just have its hands full keeping all that temporal, physical stuff, the material universe, in some sort of order with applied gravity, like a dog on a leash.

It should be recognized as self-evident that gravity is indeed the energy leash of the true deity, of that perfect law, on and within the (negative) realm of all physical. Some day, when the 'dog' dies its final temporal death, this 'leash' will haul all physical debris back in for dissolution and reabsorption into the eternal, polarity-less, perfect state. Science has already spoken on such phenomena as black holes absorbing matter—and, conversely, that "it is not inconceivable that the primal energy (of matter) emerged at zero time from quite literally nothing, uncannily in accord with the structure-less singularity described by the time-honored poetic expression: . . . without form, and void, with darkness upon the face of the deep. " * Moreover, science states: "Though it seems impossible that a particle could materialize from nothing—not even from energy***—it so happens that no laws of physics are violated . . ."**—*The violation is, instead, that of the metaphysical laws of eternity, of infinity, of the perfect state.*

So it follows that to the enlightened, returning home to the perfect state is what ultimate truth, purpose, and understanding is all about.

---

*From "Relatively Speaking," E. Chaisson, (Gen. ver. 2).
**Ibid
***The perfect state, polarity-less energy realm.

ON THE CONDITION OF RELIGIONS

Every once in a while, however rare, we experience 'prophets', enlightened beings who truly perceive the "other side"—the real, true, invisible essence—pure principle. They are soon surrounded by peripheral 'interpreters' who then build upon the backdrop of the true insight but get it distorted, wittingly or unwittingly, and depart from the deep truths, for they have not truly comprehended, understood and cognized the true reality of what their 'teacher' had meant. Then a 'religion' is created around the periphery of the full, real truth—soon with misguided, self-interested interpretation and teaching at its center.

If it were otherwise, the unbiased truth would, could, should emerge, be 'taught', pursued, be found more readily. But being prepared to give things up—power, influence, wealth, even oneself—for the higher principles is something hardly anyone is willing to do, or can do, without the real, true insight.

Apparent 'fanaticism' in the name of religion is nothing new, but if true insight were at its core and acted upon, then it would in fact no longer be fanaticism, but *delivering* adherence to cognized higher reality.

Instead, we keep on thinking and teaching, inverse to real fact and truth, that for the sake of attaining 'eternal life', we have to start out human life, human being over and over again in the physical, temporal. As stated before, eternity and infinity have no end, nor beginning—it's always there. It is something we just have to unconditionally strive for and aim to return to, abandoning our erroneous limited path on this, our physical and temporal plane. This homecoming, of course, will not be happening until and unless we have attained the higher insight and awareness.

The right place for religion is in teaching humility. Humility in the face of the perfect state, of the 'perfect God' if you will. Humility, repentance for our wanting, imperfect being—for our going counter to what we are able to perceive more and more clearly as our true alternative: metaphysical, spiritual being not amalgamated with the flesh. Churches should not be soothing, 'forgiving' comfort stations along the way in our physical life, but rather 'woodshed' stations of pain where we humbly acknowledge our accountability for our imperfection and accept our responsibility versus a perfect God— where we rise to repent our wrongs and pledge to change and seek higher, more perfect being.

This is the reality that genuine religion shall eventually have to deal with and come to teach when it attains, at last, true insight into fundamental fact and truth.

ON MAN'S SHAME

Man's shame did not come about through the legendary "temptation succumbed to," but by the dawn of his greater awareness, self-cognizance, and self-realization —left increasingly wanting in an imperfect setting. In themselves, physical processes are not out of the ordinary in nature, which our entire animal kingdom, even our plant life, 'shamelessly' attest to.

'Temptation' is a metaphoric miscue in a process that rightly has to do with nature's innate physical, basic imperfection. While it is certain that nature, once put in action by ubiquitous universal energy, evolved on its own (see molecular processes and evolutional effects in chapter "On the Categorical Judgment on the Non-cognizant Worlds")—what is happening is that man is transcending those 'innocent' natural processes *through his increasing spiritual, metaphysical awareness over his wanting, imperfect physical state of being.*

What we particularly perceive as a cause for shame is our manifestly awkward, hush-hush, dishonestly secret way of (re-)creating our imperfect being in the eyes of our truly better, decent, childlike honest judgment and innocent conscience.

In the final analysis, what we aware beings do with our awareness is what counts. *There* is our tangible opening away from imperfect being and toward our return to holiness. *There* is the true point of reckoning in the practical merits of religion, to a degree of the sciences and ultimately, of course, of philosophy.

Remember the fuss about Adam and Eve, and paradise?

ON ETERNITY AND THE TEMPORAL

It seems, in fact *it is* so simple, yet it may be doubted to the bitter end of this (temporal) world: eternity is—as is infinity—the true reality, *our* true reality, without beginning and without end, like the principle in a perfect circle. We continually *talk* about eternal life. We preach, and we sing about it in the churches. It is the center of our hopes in everything. And yet, we stand pat in our refusal to really accept the fact that *it is the only true reality*, the reality we should seek out *now*, and always.

Instead, we continue to foster and cherish the temporal, the physical, the lost. We are intrigued by time and space. Their antithesis, our real parents—eternity and infinity, the true ultimate reality in everything—we consider a fish too hard to catch and forfeit it, despite our avowed, cherished hopes and dreams about it.

We turn productive plowshares into destructive, deadly swords. We procreate, we defend the physical as if this were our salvation. We forfeit the real and true for the brief, meaningless pursuit of the temporal and the physical. All along, there is that majestic, magnificent, perfect principle of the eternal, the infinite.

As gravity, the hand of the infinite, perfect energy origin will eventually haul back *all physical phenomena*, it shall also return to that eternal origin *all temporal* by hauling in time—as *it* will have nowhere to go in the end.

Think it through, seriously—reason it out for yourself once and for all: *there* lies the rational, the reasoned principle. For the sake of our deliverance and following the principles of the true and consequential, the good, moral, and adequate in all existence: look to our home in the eternal, the infinite. Overcome self—and the temporal, imperfect, wanting physical worlds.

This philosophical finding, judgment, and conclusion is incontrovertible in light of known, cognized highest universal principles.

Once again, *all true, credible religious teaching* must eventually come together in harmonious agreement with such fundamentals if the human condition is to find its delivering answers.

ON THE NECESSITY AND ESOTERIC OF THE INQUIRY

As stated earlier, the ancient Greeks' search was more to the point of fundamental inquiry. There wasn't that much diverse, complex modern stuff to worry about and to distract them, so that with the awakening of human cognizance, they were concerned about the basics, as a virgin about virginity. Thales' motto, for example, was to "cognize, to become aware of yourself." Eastern thought is more in myths, abstract, mystical—which is not to say that there is no truth whatever in it, any more than it would be to suggest that there is no truth to the message, for example, of the Christian faith. But what should be said in all instances is that for the vast human majority, for the multitudes, the real truth is already shrouded enough and hard enough to approach and to comprehend so that it becomes harmful to the aims of the true seeker if things are made any more mythical, any more mystical than need be.

The Middle Ages through the Renaissance brought some attempts at revival of fundamental thought, albeit very peripheral (losing themselves quickly in ancient religious anchors), later though eventually culminating in the more fundamental thinking of Schopenhauer. Others, virtually to a man, were taking *the existing, the given, the here and now* largely for granted as a basis for their inquiry, and their 'findings' resulted thus more in observational commentary, definitions and 'justifications' within that scope, rather than in fundamental inquiry into basic, physical being and existence.

Modern thought is all but lost in science, technology, material pursuit, and competition. What we desperately need is a rebirth of fundamental, absolute, to-the-source-of-it-all philosophical inquiry to deal with and to cognize our true essential nature. That is still and ever our task, our challenge, as it was Thales' concern.

There are different levels on which we perceive. It is therefore not possible to make a clear statement on the true nature of things understandable to all alike. Philosophy is, then, by necessity, a selective, esoteric process. Every creature—and every one of us members of the human species—perceives, acts in accordance with the level of its true (essential) nature.

The fly in the moving railroad dining car—does it know where it is heading? Or is it just preoccupied with the crumbs, the drop of juice there on the tablecloth? Does it really have the capacity to reflect on where it is going? *Aren't most humans much the same,* cruising on planet earth—around the sun every 365 ¼ days, and turning on itself every twenty-four hours—not paying much attention to the real journey they are on; instead, just being preoccupied with the lowly pursuits of their immediate existence and gathering up their 'crumbs'—so much like the fly in the moving dining car!

It is very rare in the history of humankind that man ever *seriously, fundamentally contemplates, questions, and judges his true nature and that of all things,* as the ancient Greeks or a Schopenhauer tended to do. Instead, man has most always been, at best, just observing, analyzing, investigating, cataloguing, and speculating on that at hand—*the existing*—without much question about the underlying, *fundamental reason or rationale for it all being there in the first place,* while himself merrily pursuing, living, perpetuating nature's (wanting) course.

Small wonder, then, that after millions of years, it was only in the past few centuries that we have learned for certain which end of our world and of our solar system is up—and even despite all that newly acquired knowledge have made barely minute progress in the old Greeks' search for "what it is essentially all about, Alphy."

Unbelievably, it usually took some doing, even after actual knowledge had been gained, *to make the truth about it stick, to have it acknowledged and accepted by the old 'keepers of the faith'—the traditional establishments.* Unfortunately, it is much the same way today. The journey to genuine truth perception is a long one. And so, whatever may be revealed to some of us as *true reality* through clear insight and awareness, may not be so perceived for a long time, seemingly forever, by others not possessing the insight. But to be sure, fact and truth work inexorably, and so it will be that genuine enlightened insight shall *eventually* work its way through to our essential nature and to the true nature of all things. (See also "On Relative 'Reality', Realization and True Awareness" and "On Our Time.")

As we said, in only very few instances in millennia have a mere handful of men, sensing and being aware of the real and puzzling 'journey' we are on, *inquired fundamentally* into its apparent mystery, into their very being, into their essential nature. But our multitudes, our untold billions—not unlike all of nature's other creatures—have been going just after their own, limited objectives and physical pursuits. Yes, the little fly in the moving railroad dining car with its little crumbs over and over again. . . .

There is a challenge to our proper direction: That we make a necessity of the inquiry into ourselves, of the realization *that* we are, *who* we are, *where* we are—and to define *our origin and where we are destined.* A necessity it is indeed, if anything we are and do is to have any real meaning and purpose. Just as Thales found there to be a need to know thousands of years ago, so should we now in our higher awareness resolve to pursue the inquiry—to its final conclusion.

Is religion a necessity? It certainly can, or should be, to the human soul and intuition that realize something is incomplete in a cognizant, aware, knowing existence without a tangible 'higher' consequence than just its physical, temporal, mortal "fact of being."

However, let that old-time religion not go off on tangents. Let it be an independent, cognizant, live and *knowing belief and faith in real truth.* What we must come home to is *a belief system that recognizes that which is true and factual.* Commonly, to 'believe' something somehow implies *'not knowing'*, therefore it should be 'believed'—without foundation *in fact.* This premise of 'blind faith' on mushy and murky grounds is so terribly wrong and divisive.

Let us believe in a central theme of what is real and true, and *known to be so.* Why should something not be the object of 'belief' *just because it proves, in fact, true?* Let's remove the wrong notion that if we are to be "believers," we must cling to something that is shrouded in myth, something lacking the factual, the tangible, the real—"that's why we must believe and accept it as faith." Let good old common-sense folklore help us out here that says: *"Seeing is believing!"* *Believing reality* is a big step toward true cognizance.

The inquisitors were so bent on "their belief, their faith," that they denied reality and true fact even after they were known—and known for centuries before the wrong was recanted. We must not ever let that be repeated.

REFLECTIONS

In our constant struggle over physical and economic survival, we do not get to think and reflect much about our fundamental being and values.

But then, it has been pretty much that way all along. The entire animal kingdom, including man, has always instinctively acted and procreated full of preoccupation with survival and security (feeling more secure with protective young around rather than being, and ending up, alone). This instinct is quite normal, all else being equal and of purpose and rationality. But what if that turns out in the ultimate to be erroneous—at base without good, valid purpose or rationality? What if our physical life, and all physical existence turn out to be, in truth, wrong—*"sinful,"* as our very life source *is in fact depicted in religious narratives*—what if the gist of the story of Eve and the Apple turns out to be the quintessential, unqualified spiritual truth champion?

What if our needle's-eye birth passage through the demeaning, secretive physical source of our imperfect being is our constant and ultimate test of consent to our life's imperfection, of our will to continue on as we are? What then?

In ultimate consequence, the uncompromising metaphysical laws of perfection, of infinity and eternity leave no doubt that it is, in fact, so.

But then again, as related in our "Holy Book," unawareness is fairly a rational defense against direct responsibility, against guilt; the point being that as long as we are without the awareness, we go among the blind—while nonetheless carrying the burden, bearing the (negative) consequences of the low life. Meanwhile, though, in man's condition of not (yet) being fully and consciously aware of the higher option, his unawareness does in fact help ease his burden of the low life struggle, as the latter is unwittingly accepted and not questioned fundamentally at this stage. With the attainment of higher awareness, however, we shall grow more cognizant of our imperfection and come to bear the responsibility of seeking to transcend and getting delivered from physical affliction, readying for more perfect being in closer harmony with higher universal principles.

Stepping back a bit—in our human predicament, given our advanced development, doesn't it in large part come down to the basic fact that man simply relishes and believes in his little sand-castle life that (he thinks) is his to control and that he wants to—or in his lack of higher awareness erroneously thinks he needs to—pass on as a means toward reaching a perceived higher purpose? But he thereby in fact misses his homecoming, denies himself his deliverance, the very objective he purports to be pursuing.

We can assume, can't we, that the human species is the most accomplished among earth's creatures? It has managed to tinker with the very guts of physics, such as the atom. It is capable, through its intelligence, to comprehend the very base of physics' makeup, *to manipulate it, and to use it for negative purposes.* But now think for a moment: would a perfect God intend to have that happen?

Yes, think about it!

Why then would a perfect God create infernos like churning, burning stars, let the stuff cool, and have ignorant little physical creatures be evolved there to suffer and fight, to 'feed off of' one another (read food chain), then soon to perish—only to be reborn, on and on in a seemingly useless, helter-skelter cycle?

Yes, think it through to the ultimate, rational conclusion.

It certainly makes more sense to attribute such physical entrapments, all physical manifestation and phenomena, to a negative power—to be overcome by a cognizant, righteous, positive spirit and awareness. In the last analysis, that must be our ultimate judgment on the true nature and rationale of the physical universe, as I am sure it is a perfect God's. Enlightened awareness and understanding of true, incontrovertible higher principles tell us that, without any doubt.

Who could contend unequivocally that a much greater negative power (than our own that created our awesome nuclear bombs) could not tinker with things on an immensely grander, 'cosmic' scale, creating the physical universe as we know it, when all should have been left in the infinite, eternal, perfect state? Try to visualize such a greater power exiting a much more massive 'Garden of Eden', as it were. If you can fathom that, then you may just be on to something on the way toward understanding the mystery of our imperfect existence.

The overall negation of the physical state is a philosophical judgment and decision that must be made categorically (see also "On the Categorical Judgment on the Non-Cognizant Worlds"). But it surely need not mean that we should immediately cease taking proper care of our physical body, or quit using our motor car and electric energy because they may cause unhealthy air, or not eat certain foods because it may be repugnant to feed upon other creatures in nature. As long as we exist in this, our imperfect state, we have little choice but to live it out as best we can—*in quiet humility.* Flesh somehow will consume flesh to the point of salvation, of deliverance from the flesh. And you may have heard it before: "It is not important what goes in the mouth, but rather what comes from it."

The important thing is that we undertake those tangible steps our higher awareness tells us to take, which is to strive for perfection and not to keep re-creating and reliving the imperfect state. That is reasonable, rational, and in tune with our true, moral conscience and enlightened self-cognizance. That is in fact the prevailing of, the conquest by the enlightened spirit over our body-selves; the overcoming of our physical amalgamation, affliction—the deliverance of our heightened subconscious essence from its present imperfect, lower energy state.

Voices have been heard. Probably not much understood or comprehended, but *heard*—in some instances over and over, even for millennia. Prophets and philosophers have laid out their cards, sometimes fairly comprehensively—to not much avail. It is as if the human species for some reason or another, from its very edge of ultimate understanding and salvation, is putting up the greatest resistance, a solid wall, against its own deliverance.

It appears evident, then, that our species does not (yet) possess the real self-cognizance that could deliver it—the full awareness it would take to abandon its crude, imperfect ship for the higher, more perfect state.

We must, therefore, see our purpose, our mission in teaching and gaining the higher awareness, the self-cognizance and self-realization needed to overcome ourselves and reach purer, higher status.

"Give us your children for the first six years, and we shall keep them forever" is what we must wrest from the prevalent religions. What we need is no more than to just keep the minds of the young *open,* so that they can make up their own minds, render their own decisions—unhindered by early indoctrination, doubt, fear, intimidation, even institutional delusion, but solely by their own deliberation and free will—once they are ready to do so. Not too much asking, is it? Perhaps the churches, for their own purposes, borrowed from Socrates, who is quoted as having said: "Pay attention to the very young and make the best of them."

Societies have for the most part been willing to "hang their hats, their souls" on often vague, even wacky religions for ultimate answers. Now let us for a change embark on a *rational, moral resolve* of our human situation, based on all reliable factors available to us.

But I want to caution you: it is hard to imagine what a sea of protest, of opposition and disgust will come to rise on the part of a species—and its establishments—that has been so thoroughly indoctrinated, that thinks it is so wonderful, "created in the very image of the perfect, infinite, eternal God." Yet in fact, in purely *physical makeup,* when we look closely enough, where are we basically so different from other species: monkey, cat, dog, cattle—you name it, having the same basic design and structure: legs, head, eyes, nostrils, teeth, ears, and digestive system . . .? The difference, obviously, is in our consciousness, in our mental, metaphysical attributes in the direction of processes that are increasingly alien to the strictly physical, sand-castle aspects of our species, *the direction in which we should be looking and going* in pursuit of "likeness to God": spiritual, infinite, eternal orientation and rebirth—not physical and temporal.

We must remove the mystery around the human phenomenon. As there are birds to fly if there was air, and fish to swim if there was water, rational thought and reason(ing) were bound to evolve if there was a rational principle out there. And if we do not concede as surely as water seeking to go to the bottom that when conditions are right for things to evolve *they will evolve motivated by reigning universal energy principles,* then we open ourselves up to all kinds of mysterious theories and belief systems, speculation, superstition and hypocrisy. For we are becoming so overwhelmed by "the miracle of it all—and of ourselves"—that we forfeit rational, logical thinking and give in to irrational processes.

To be sure, considerable reservations about the (often wayward) ways in actual practices notwithstanding, religious belief is inherently very beneficial. We must only take care to look for the good and true in it and sort out the unreal, hypocritical, erroneous and superstitious—to render the field fertile for real, true, *knowing belief and faith.* (See chapter "On the God Concept").

ON NATURE AND THE OBJECT WORLD

If our physical being, our material amalgamation, our imperfect affliction is by our own doing, by our own guilt, our sin—how, why then are there plants, beautiful trees, "life" come about, apparently, *without "sin"—by nature's inanimate and non-cognizant processes alone? No causal, conscious "cardinal sins" involved?—The Grand Canyon "just happened," nobody dug it according to an architect's or engineer's plans and specifications . . . ?*

Well, did it?

The explanation lies in the bigger scheme of things. We have to go back at large to the original cause, back to the 'irrational principle' of physical phenomenon. Under ultimate, highest principles, eternity and infinity have it. So whatever occurred and is occurring, and whatever will for whatever reason occur that does not measure up to those pure, highest principles, *let it alone philosophically—* it is not the real thing, true reality. We can be sure of it.

Temporal, physical phenomenon in any form simply is not consequential in light of ultimate, eternal principles. It can only satisfy some temporal, wanting force, will, or urge—serving innately imperfect aims and limited purpose, *no matter what the magnitude of the enterprise,* up to and including what we conceive to be the entire physical, temporal universe.

Enlightened cognizance and truly attained self-realization make that clear beyond any shadow of doubt.

ON THE CATEGORICAL JUDGMENT ON THE NON-COGNIZANT WORLDS

Our categorical judgment on the 'bigger picture' non-cognizant, temporal, physical universe has to be one of error, fallacy, and shortcoming since we know unequivocally that if there is a *perfect God's rational principle, its fundamental nature is infinite and eternal* (and if there weren't such a rational principle, where would we find the promise and rationale of a 'perfect God' to save us from the meaningless abyss?). Our enduring religions, and foremost our deepest inner intuitions, speak to that from earliest times. There simply can be no doubt about it. Only forces intent on perpetuating the fallacy of the temporal, of the finite physical could disagree with these most basic and all-encompassing truth principles. And so it follows that the same (negative) powers that created the temporal, the physical in the first place, are still at work recreating, reenacting their erroneous 'creation'. Metaphorically, it identifies with man's departure and continuing absence from the Garden of Eden, as it were.

The workings and explanation of molecular processes should not cause us that much puzzlement. Once
impurity, spatial dust, physical phenomenon, and thereby
friction and polarity were occurring, the one-on-one
game of positive and negative, of attract or reject, and
magnetism were in business—and the molecular processes followed consequentially. Driven by ubiquitous
universal energy, *molecular multiplication* evolved plant
and life forms in accordance with prevailing environmental conditions. Our grasp of mathematics can help us out
here for a better understanding, with its basic principles
applied to such foundations of matter and life forms as
atoms, molecules, DNA, genes, and the natural elements.
Nature's processes then, simply put, are but applied practical manifestations of (mutating) 'mathematical multiplication principia'—given certain environments, and
conditions, corresponding evolutionary effects would occur.

To avoid the suspicion of oversimplification here, let
us look at our solar system as an illustration: guided by
the universal energy principle of gravity, all of its manifestations, as they occurred on scales large and small,
evolved into a precise orbital environment—perfectly
balanced, as is the case with the entire universe.

So it is that guided by those strong, controlling universal energy principles, water would go to the bottom
and, under the many different environmental conditions,
there would be birds to fly if there was air, and fish to
swim if there was water. The mystery is considerably di-

minished and our view of evolutional effects reaffirmed when we observe a fish out of water, or a drowning mouse trying in vain for dry ground. Every facet of nature has its proper place, and only in its proper place and environment will it thrive. (See also "Reflections.")

To be sure, the process' guiding principles are not by our bench marks, our standards of reference, perception and understanding—further evidence that kangaroo newborn, finding its pouch outside the mother's belly for its final development. Or that bird, that whale, finding their winter homes far away through the air or under water, or yet that spider, doing its architectural masterwork. Our own lack of "natural instincts" and our inept vantage point for understanding these phenomena are as much evident as they are irrelevant to these attributes of the natural processes.

A brief synopsis of the 'universal bigger picture' concerning the object and temporal worlds, then, would go something like this: overall, we have an impure, imperfect *negative* 'bigger power' behind the temporal and physical origins; we have physical phenomena occurring; we have physical "life" evolving, eventually culminating in self-cognizant, self-realizing being that will ultimately recognize its misplacement in an erroneous, temporal, physical world and 'long to go home' to its true origin—original, eternal, polarity-less, perfect state energy.

So we have in fact two negations to affirm in the final resolution of our plight, for our philosophical and spiritual deliverance: the renunciation of our own physical being, and the categorical negation of all physical phenomena as a whole for being solid manifestations of impurity and imperfection.

This is an *inevitable, rational philosophical overview,* for we know that ultimate consequence—eternity and infinity—*cannot* have anything to do with the temporal and physical as an end in itself.

CONCLUDING REMARKS

Even though, in this age of 'higher education', this is a lay effort—the truth, the facts are solid and intact. Details are often not to be had (as in Zen)—but if you read carefully, you will catch the message. *It's all there to put together a true, ultimate perspective about our life, about ourselves, and "our" universe.* There is only one caveat: that you be ready for it—for seeking, grasping, and accepting the delivering truth.

If I were to offer some suggestions on just how to go about tangibly reaching one's 'Paranirvana', I would have to remind you that there are no specific, concrete directions to be had. You don't turn left by the third traffic light and then to the right on the next corner. We are dealing with "understanding of the infinite, the eternal"—God, if you will. Invisible, formless; "Thou shalt not make an image of God" may still best explain the proper understanding of these principles. The moment you try to visualize this ethereal ultimateness in time, through form, matter or presence, you lose its heart—its true core concept.

You must start with a good dose of humility about

yourself. Take yourself out of the picture. Always keep in mind, always concentrate, meditate on the ultimate goal, on the ultimate objective: the timeless, formless, non-physical—no trivia, no trinkets, *only your cherished principles, moving away from the material, physical, and temporal domains toward that which is eternal, infinite, moral, true and rational.*

Now, as a concluding thought, I need to ask:

Which of our other disciplines: Science, Religion—or Hocus-Pocus?—is in any legitimate, valid position to disclaim what we found to be our deepest philosophical answers and conclusions?

Think about it, seriously.

Science has no conscience, and its domain ends with the bounds of the physical, the temporal.

Religion, dogmatized, has its feet off the ground and much of its head in the sand.

How, then, could anything but *serious philosophic reflection* lead us rationally to the *depths of ultimate fact and truth, to the way things really are?*

May the blessings of full enlightenment and understanding come to you and lead you to deliverance.

Farewell,

—SOMOS

P.S. I trust you have observed that this is not the usual 'philosophical discourse'—the rehashing of 'philosophy'—of "what he said . . . and he said . . . and what he said" once upon a time. Rather, it is intended as a straightforward, contemporary judgment on universal accountability, an encouragement to seek out that which is truly and forever consequential, and to look for our ultimate fulfillment, for our deliverance, *now*. What good is it to postpone, to defer our human deliverance from generation to generation, once our consciousness, our awareness have glimpsed the higher ground?

So watch, my friend, as your neighbor walks his lovely dog every day—and reflect on whether *you* are that much better off? The distinguishing, telling difference lies not in our modern mechanical flush, but in the recognition of our own imperfect state of being, and in the acceptance of a higher metaphysical reality that is out there as surely as the invisible, infinite—call it the pure, 'divine' eternal energy that is manifest by the eternal law, and reach, of gravity.

And yes, one last point, in an ongoing true 'reality check':

We must use constant vigilance in keeping with our gained cognizance and awareness because—remember it well from temptation—"the devil always wants you back."

APPENDIX

The Roman Empire

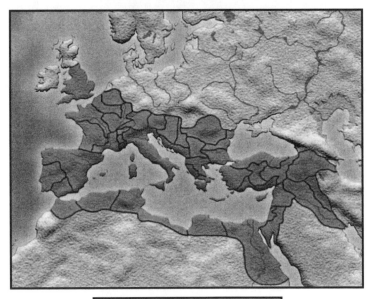

The Roman Empire in AD 116
The empire at its largest extent

Annexation of Alpes Cottiae - AD 64/65
Annexation of the Agri Decumates - 74
Division of Moesia into two provinces in about AD 85; superior (upper) and inferior (lower)
Annexation of the kingdom of Nabatea as Province of Arabia Petra - AD 105 or 106
Conquest of Dacia - AD 106
Division of Pannonia into two provinces in AD 107; superior (upper) and inferior (lower)
Annexation of Armenia - AD 114
Conquest of Mesopotamia - AD 116
Conquest of Assyria - AD 116

The preceding geographical map illustrates the expanse of the Roman empire in its prime with its unquenchable thirst for power and, for better or for worse, its consequent influence on the development of Western civilization.

✳

Could the emerging Christian movement really have been able to remain true to its intended spiritual cause while under the auspices and control of vile emperors of the time, capable of committing such unfathomable, untold atrocities as the burning of human beings at the stake, the live crucifixion of Jesus and of thousands of other human beings who would not blindly follow the empire's edicts?

In accepting Christianity as legitimate religion of the state, combining the power and influence of the Roman empire with the early Christian church, emperor Constantine hoped to engender secret mystical powers in his battles. (We see this state/faith relationship in military actions very much alive to this day.)

But should we rightly believe that Jesus would have wanted his spiritual message to be hijacked and contaminated for the benefit of a 'unified partnership' with the state, out to conquer and defend territories for the Roman empire?—Think about it!

When divergent religious hierarchies start fighting one another over their respective concepts of God and faith—irrational as that may be in itself—their true, hidden motivation really lies in the domination and control of human civilizations, and whenever that comes to pass, humanity is headed for very troubled times. Thus, instead of offering providence and hope, our religions may be made to cause great harm, hate, havoc and despair.

The Christian cause needs fundamental reform in purity to become true to its spiritual calling, as does the Islamic religion that itself emanated from belief in Jesus' spiritual message.